DATE DUE

| | | | |
|---|---|---|---|
| APR 8 1987 | OCT 16 1995 | | |
| MAY 7 - 1987<br>JUN 9 1987 | NOV 6 1995 | | |
| JAN 11 1988 | JUL 21 1999 | | |
| FEB 18 1988 | AUG 10 1998 | | |
| APR 23 1988 | JAN 13 2004<br>DEC 29 2004 | | |
| JUN 30 1988 | | | |
| JUN 8 - 1989 | MAR 12 2005 | | |
| FEB 9 - 1990 | MAR 05 2012<br>JAN 27 2014 | | |
| APR 9 - 1990 | | | |
| JUL 13 1990 | JUL 16 2015 | | |
| JUN 5 1991 | | | |
| JUN 5 - 1991<br>AUG 7 1991 | | | |
| | | | |

MARTIN J. GUTNIK

# SIMPLE ELECTRICAL DEVICES

A GROLIER COMPANY
FRANKLIN WATTS
NEW YORK ▪ LONDON ▪ TORONTO ▪ SYDNEY
A FIRST BOOK ▪ 1986

Diagrams by Vantage Art, Inc.

Photographs courtesy of:
New York Public Library Picture Collection: p. 2;
Bakken Library of Electricity in Life: p. 8;
Radio Shack/Tandy Corporation: pp. 27, 57 (top left);
General Electric: pp. 36, 46;
The Bettmann Archive: p. 52;
A T & T Bell Laboratories: p. 57 (left and top right);
A T & T Bell Technologies: p. 57 (bottom right).

Library of Congress Cataloging in Publication Data
Gutnik, Martin J.
Simple electrical devices.

(A First book)
Bibliography: p.
Includes index.
Summary: Descriptions and experiments introduce and explain electrical cells, batteries, and other simple electric devices.
1. Electric apparatus and appliances—Juvenile literature. 2. Electricity—Experiments—Juvenile literature. [1. Electric apparatus and appliances. 2. Electricity—Experiments. 3. Experiments] I. Title.
TK148.G88 1986 621.3 85-26369
ISBN 0-531-10127-4


Printed in the United States of America
6 5 4 3 2 1

# CONTENTS

# SIMPLE ELECTRICAL DEVICES

In loving memory
of my father,
Max Gutnik

# INTRODUCTION

In this book you will learn some of the history and development of electrical devices. You also will have a chance to perform some of the famous experiments in electricity and magnetism and to build some simple electrical devices.

In experimenting and building, you will be following in the footsteps of the great inventors and scientists of the past. You are encouraged to ask the kinds of questions that may lead you, too, to some new discoveries. You also will be introduced to such modern electrical devices as TVs, telephones, and computer chips.

Many of the experiments in this book deal with electrical devices powered by batteries. *Although the batteries are not powerful enough to cause severe electric shocks, you must still be careful not to burn yourself on hot wires.* Use the batteries only as directed.

You will be building devices that require the use of simple tools and ordinary materials. Make sure you have on hand a hammer, electrical pliers, tweezers, screwdriver, electrical tape, wire cutter, scissors, 100-foot (30-m) roll of bell wire, and 1.5-volt dry cell. These should be available at hardware and electrical supply stores.

*Magnetic car used in China in the third century B.C.E.*
*The statue's arm contained a magnet and always pointed south.*

# 1

# MAGNETISM AND STATIC ELECTRICITY

Electricity and magnetism are so entwined that we must begin our exploration of electrical devices with the story of a simple magnetic device—the compass.

## MAGNETISM AND THE COMPASS

Iron has been known to people since approximately 4000 B.C.E. (before the common era, or first century). Among the various types of iron ore is magnetite, a dark, shiny, crystal-like material.

On occasion, pieces of magnetite are found that are permanently magnetized, that is, able to attract and repel other objects. These pieces of magnetite are known as **lodestones.**

Lodestones were discovered in an area of the world called Magnesia. Some say the word "magnet" was derived from the word Magnesia. Others believe the term comes from Magnes, the name of a shepherd who discovered that the lodestone attracts iron objects. Some scientists believe that people knew about the attractive, or magnetic, powers of the lodestone as early as 3000 B.C.E.

There are many stories of the early use of lodestones in China. By 2000 B.C.E., the Chinese knew of these magnetic materials and used them. Among the discoveries credited to the Chinese is the compass, probably the first magnetic device. In approximately 1000 B.C.E., the Chinese learned that if a lodestone and steel needle were rubbed together, the lodestone would permanently magnetize the needle. Since the magnetic needle always pointed in the same direction, the Chinese used the needles to keep them from getting lost while traveling. The needles served as the first compasses.

Europeans started using the magnetic compass in the mid-thirteenth century. The Europeans probably learned of the compass from the Arabs, and the Arabs likely learned about the instrument from the Chinese.

## PROJECT 1:
## A HOMEMADE COMPASS

MATERIALS

steel sewing needle
bar magnet
two or three steel pins
aluminum pan
cork (from bottle)
pocket compass

Change your sewing needle into a temporary magnet by rubbing it across one end of the bar magnet. Slowly rub the needle forty times over one pole of the bar magnet. After each stroke of the needle, remove it from the magnet.

Test your needle to see if it is a magnet by attempting to pick up the pins with the needle. If the needle attracts the pins, it is magnetized (a magnet). If it does not, it probably needs more stroking. If the needle is still not magnetized, use a different bar magnet.

Once the needle is magnetized, push it through a cork. Fill the pan with water and float the cork in the water. Put the pocket compass next to the pan. Check the needle to see if it points in the same direction as the compass. In what direction is it pointing? Why? Twist the needle a quarter turn. Let go. What happens? Why?

# STATIC ELECTRICITY

In ancient Greece, about 2,500 years ago, a philosopher-scientist named Thales discovered that **amber,** or fossilized tree sap, could pick up light objects, such as bits of grass or feathers, when rubbed with an object like fur. For a long time afterward, many scientists thought the attractive powers of lodestone and amber were both due to magnetism.

In 1600, the English scientist William Gilbert explained that the force possessed by rubbed amber was not magnetism. He explained that a compass needle lined up in the north-south direction because the Earth itself was a magnet. Gilbert then presented his ideas on why amber attracts and repels certain materials.

Amber, Gilbert said, "electrified" these materials, which caused them to be attracted to the amber. Our modern-day word "electricity" comes from the Greek word *elektron,* a word that means "amber."

We now know that the force which causes rubbed amber to attract or repel certain objects is **static electricity.** Friction between a piece of fur and a piece of amber transfers electrons from atoms in the fur to atoms in the amber. **Electrons** are the negatively charged parts of atoms, and **atoms** are the building blocks of matter.

Because the amber has gained electrons, it becomes negatively charged. When another negatively charged object is brought near the amber, it is repelled. But when a positively charged object is brought near the amber, it is attracted to the amber. These actions follow what is known as the **law of electrostatics:** *Like* charges repel each other; *unlike* charges attract each other.

So, although Thales was the first person to record observations of static electricity in action, Gilbert was the first to properly call this force electricity. But even though Gilbert was right in saying that electricity and magnetism are different kinds of forces, you will see in chapters to come how closely related these forces actually are. In fact, it is their close relationship that is so important in the development of electrical devices.

## PROJECT 2:
## THE LAW OF ELECTROSTATICS

MATERIALS

comb
several pieces of paper

Run a comb through your hair quickly. Do this eight or nine times. Now hold the comb over several small scraps of paper. What happens? How does this event comply with the law of electrostatics?

Run the comb through your hair again. Turn on the water faucet and adjust the valve until you get a slow, even stream coming from the tap. Hold the comb close to the stream of running water. What happens? Why? How does this event comply with the law of electrostatics?

# 2

# EARLY ELECTRICAL DEVICES

After 1600, research and experimentation in electricity increased. People became very interested in electricity and wanted to learn more about it.

William Gilbert and Robert Boyle both discovered that electricity was created when a solid piece of sulfur was rubbed with a cloth. Otto von Guericke, the mayor of Magdeburg, took Gilbert's and Boyle's discoveries and went a step further. He made a large ball of sulfur and mounted it on a rod held up by a wooden frame. He spun the ball of sulfur with a crank and held a piece of soft cloth against the ball while it rotated. When he pressed the cloth against the ball, sparks shot out. Von Guericke also discovered that electricity attracts and repels certain objects.

When von Guericke held a feather close to a charged sulfur globe in a machine he invented, the feather was attracted to the ball until they touched. Upon touching the globe, the feather was repelled and floated above the globe.

In 1729, Stephen Gray, an Englishman, discovered how to transmit an electric charge, or make electric charges move. This was an important discovery for the future of electrical devices, for an electrical device needs moving charges in order to operate.

An *electrical device* is any object that uses electricity to function. Von Guericke's electrical machine was an electrical device, because the static electricity produced caused the attractive and repulsive forces.

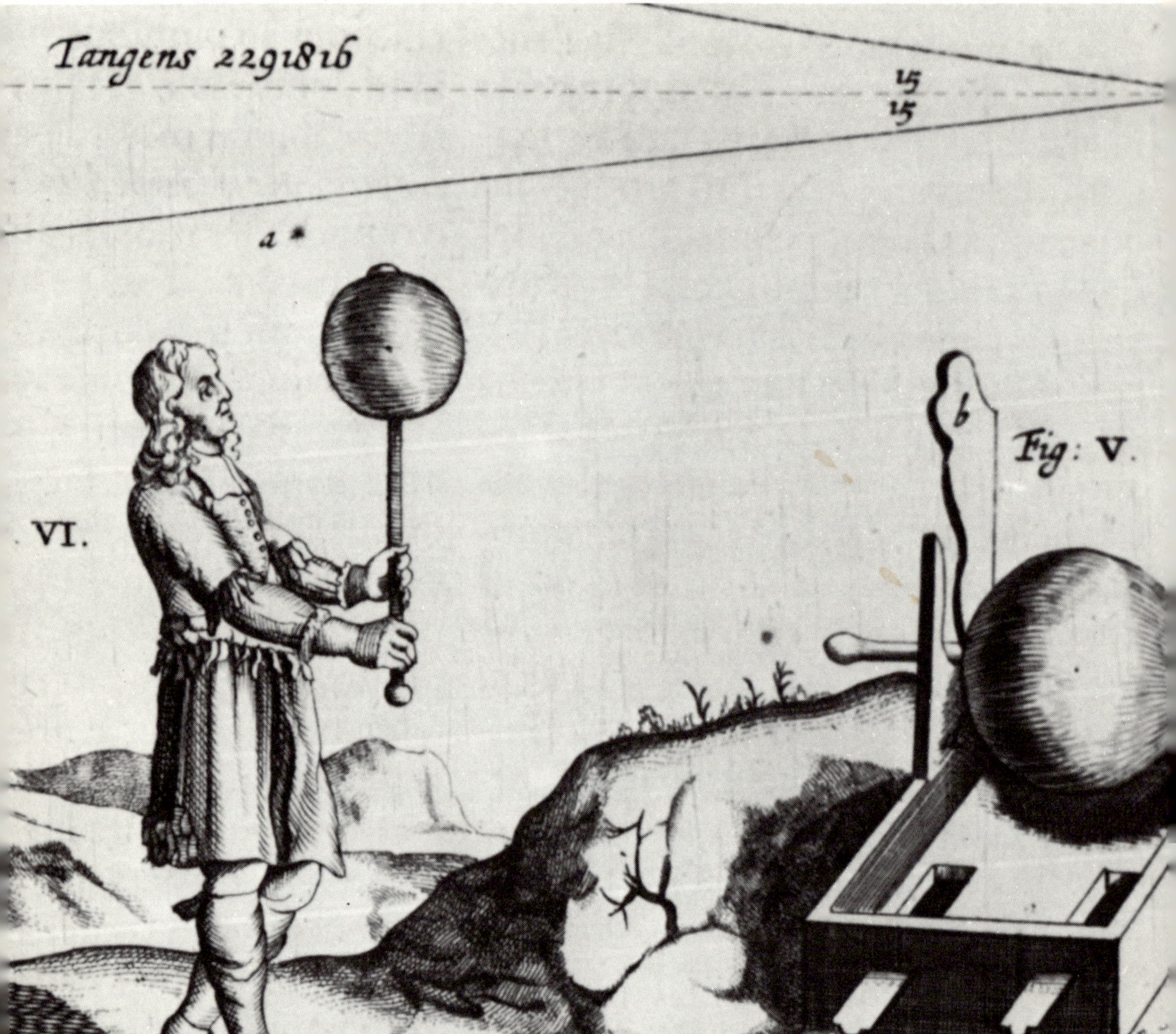


*Otto von Guericke's 17th-century electric generator. It looks quite a bit different from today's electric generators, don't you think?*

Gray performed many experiments attempting to electrify, or give an electric charge to, different metals. Somehow he came upon the idea of using an electrified glass. The electrified tube, he thought, would transfer its electric charge to metals. When he tested his idea, he found it to be true. He transferred an electric charge from a glass tube to iron rods by using a wire. Gray was one of the first scientists to use wires as electrical conductors. A **conductor** is any material that will transmit an electric charge.

Charles Du Fay, a French scientist, showed that all objects could be electrified. He also discovered the existence of two kinds of electricity: static and current. Static electricity, as you have learned, is electricity created by friction when certain objects are rubbed together. **Current electricity** is electrons moving through a conductor.

## THE LEYDEN JAR

After Du Fay's discoveries, many scientists experimented with electricity, attempting to make improvements in the electrical devices of the time. In 1746, E. G. von Kliest, a German scientist, invented the **Leyden jar.** The first Leyden jar was a bottle partially filled with water and containing a metal rod, which could hold an electric charge. Soon after, it was discovered that a bottle lined and covered with tinfoil would hold an electric charge equally as well as the Leyden jar. This discovery led to the understanding that the electricity was stored in the glass, not in the water.

## GALVANI AND ANIMAL ELECTRICITY

Luigi Galvani (1737–1798) was a professor of anatomy at the University of Bologna, in Italy. Galvani had an electrical device in his laboratory which he used to study the effects of electric shocks on animals and people. Galvani believed that electricity might be a cure for some human diseases.

One day, as Galvani was working with the leg of a frog, he noticed that the leg moved every time his electrical machine sparked. Galvani found this quite interesting and performed experiments trying to prove that electricity was in the muscles or nerves of the frog.

## THE VOLTAIC PILE

In 1800, Count Alessandro Volta (1745–1827) announced to the world that he had invented a chemical source of electricity, what we now call a battery. All the other sources up until then had been mechanical. He called his battery a **voltaic pile.** Volta's battery was a source of **electromotive force (EMF),** the force that pushes electrons.

Electrons move from an area where they are in excess to an area of fewer electrons. EMF pushes the electrons. The electrons move away from the source of the EMF to an area with fewer electrons. We usually measure EMF as voltage. The unit is the **volt.**

The Electrical Age was now in full swing. Volta's discovery led to more extensive experiments in electricity. Soon devices were invented that could light buildings and power cities.

## PROJECT 3:
## AN ELECTROSCOPE

By building an electroscope, you can repeat Du Fay's experiments which showed that all objects can be electrified.

MATERIALS

wooden stick or broom handle about 3′ (1 m) long
masking tape
two 12″ (30-cm) pieces of silk thread

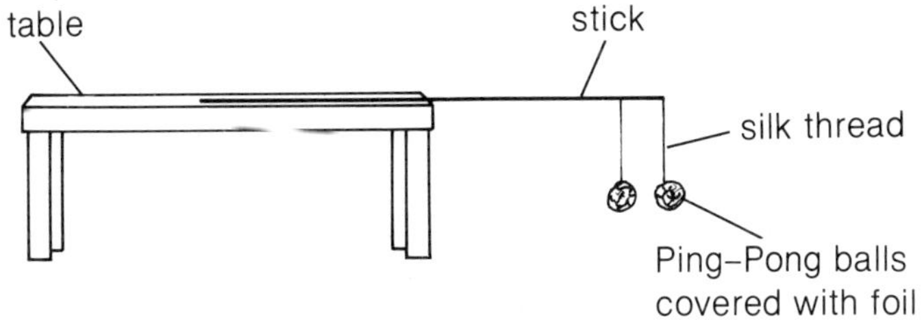


Fig. 1. Diagram of the electroscope to be built in Project 3

2 Ping-Pong balls
two 8″ × 8″ (20 × 20-cm) pieces of aluminum foil
comb
piece of glass (make sure there are no sharp edges)
silk cloth

Secure the stick or broom handle on top of a table, with about 18 inches (46 cm) of the stick extended over the edge. Tape one end of each silk thread to each Ping-Pong ball and cover each ball with the aluminum foil. Tie the other end of the silk thread to the part of the stick hanging over the edge of the table. The two balls should now be hanging freely over the edge. See Fig. 1.

Slide the thread on the stick until the two balls are almost touching each other. Your electroscope is now ready for use. It will detect the presence of electricity and react differently to different kinds of electricity.

For your first experiment, run the comb through your hair several times. Make sure the comb makes contact with each ball in turn and that your fingers do not touch the Ping-Pong balls. What happens?

Now, in order to remove the electric charge, touch each Ping-Pong ball with your fingers. This done, rub a silk cloth over a piece of glass, and then touch the cloth to each ball. What happens?

Again, remove the electric charge by touching the Ping-Pong balls with your fingers. Move the strings several inches apart on the stick. Touch one ball with the comb and the other with the cloth. What happens?

The comb you ran through your hair gained electrons from your hair. Because the comb gained electrons, it became negatively charged. The silk cloth lost electrons when it was rubbed on the glass. Because the cloth lost electrons, it became positively charged. This is a good example of the law of electrostatics.

# 3

# ELECTRIC CIRCUITS

In order to further understand the nature of electrical devices, you will need to know how electric **circuits** work. All electrical devices use circuits. Some circuits are simple; some circuits are quite complicated.

An electric circuit is the path that electrons follow from the source of a current to a device and back to the source. To put it another way, a circuit is a loop in which a current flows from start to finish. Circuits are necessary to keep an electric current flowing. The EMF keeps the current flowing by pushing electrons along the path of the circuit.

As an electric current moves through a circuit, it meets resistance from the conductor. **Resistance** is a property of material that inhibits the flow of electricity. Resistance is like friction. The longer the electrons must travel through a conductor, the greater the resistance. The thinner the conductor, the closer the electrons and, thus, the greater the resistance. The greater the resistance, the smaller the current that can pass through a conductor.

In 1826, Georg Simon Ohm formulated a law to measure electrical resistance. This law, which bears his name, is called **Ohm's law.** Ohm discovered that the current, voltage, and resistance in an electric circuit are all related. For a fixed resistance, as the voltage increases, the current increases proportionally. The formula for Ohm's law is still used today.

## COMPLETE AND BROKEN CIRCUITS

Most of the circuits and devices described in this book use a battery as a source of EMF. Another common source is a **generator.**

Complete circuits are found in all electrical devices, from radios, to televisions, to computers, to spaceships. Let us look at various types of circuits so that we can then build our own. This will also help us to better understand the various electrical devices and how they work. (Before reading further, take a look at Fig. 2, which shows some of the symbols used in diagrams of circuits.)

The source of EMF for the circuit shown in Fig. 3 is a battery. Electrons flow from the battery to the light bulb. They flow into the bulb and encounter resistance from a thin wire inside the bulb called a **filament.** The filament glows because resistance creates heat. An analogy is a bicycle brake: When you apply the brake, the friction, or resistance, slows down the bike; at the same time, the brake will

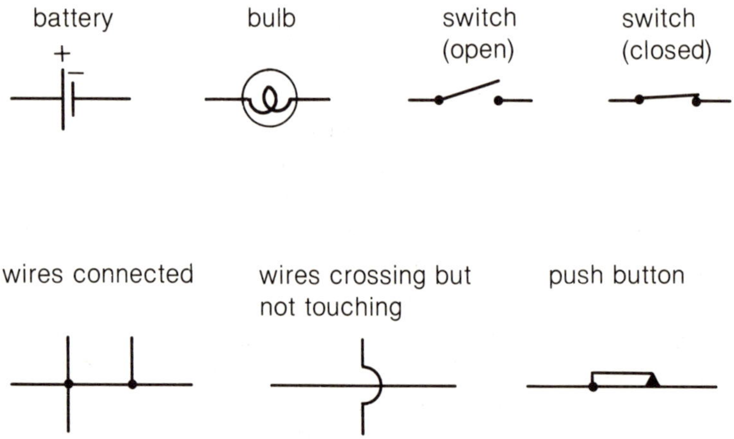


Fig. 2. The symbols used in diagramming electric circuits

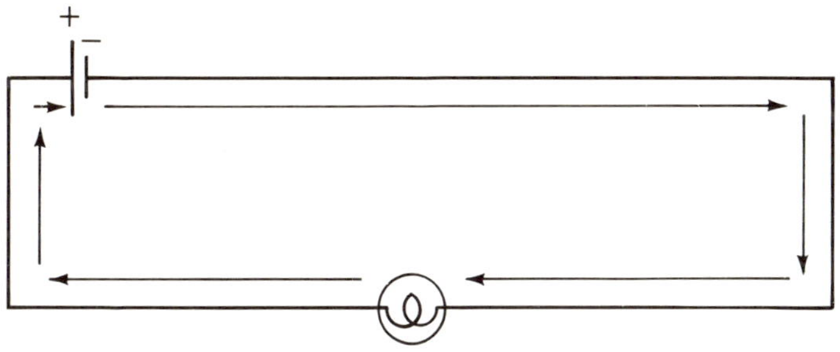


Fig. 3. In a complete circuit, diagrammed here, the bulb lights up. The arrows show the flow of electrons.

grow hot. The electrons continue moving out of the bulb and back to the battery.

A functioning circuit must be complete. If any part of a circuit is broken, the circuit will not function. The electrons must be able to travel from start to finish. If the wire were repaired in the broken circuit shown in Fig. 4, the electrons would once again be able to flow and the bulb would light up.

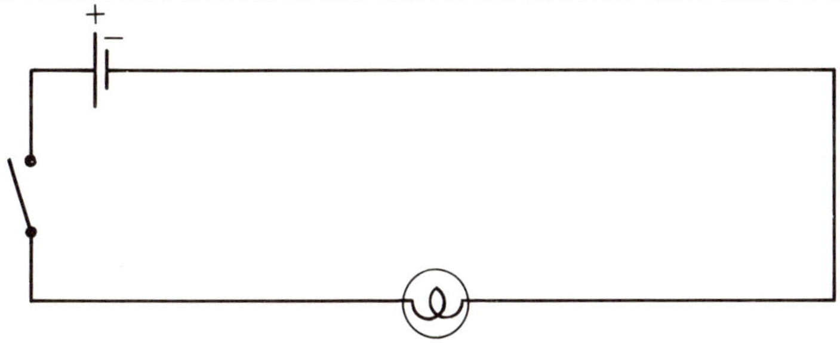


Fig. 4. This drawing shows a broken circuit, in which the electrons cannot flow from start to finish. The bulb does not light.

## PROJECT 4:
A COMPLETE CIRCUIT

MATERIALS

3′ (1 m) of bell wire
6-volt dry cell battery
porcelain receptacle for the bulb
6-volt light bulb

Strip the plastic **insulator** (a material that interrupts electrical flow) off both ends of two strands of wire, each about 18 inches (46 cm) long. Attach one strand to the positive pole (anode) of your dry cell battery. Attach the other end of the wire to the porcelain receptacle.

Next attach the other wire to the negative pole (**cathode**) of the battery. Run this wire to the other screw on the receptacle and attach it. Screw the 6-volt light bulb into the receptacle. What happens? Why?

## CLOSED AND OPEN CIRCUITS

The complete circuit that you made is really a **closed circuit.** Since most circuits have switches, a closed circuit is the name given to the system when the switch is closed and the electrons can freely travel from start to finish.

When the switch is opened, the circuit is broken and the electrons cannot travel from start to finish. This is called an **open circuit.**

An electric light switch, the kind you will find in any room of your home, opens and closes a circuit. Circuits are also opened and closed by switches on most electrical devices such as televisions, washing machines, computers, and stereo receivers. Can you find any devices around your house or apartment that have no switches?

## SERIES CIRCUITS

A **series circuit** (Fig. 5) includes two or more electrical devices connected by a single path. For these devices to work, the current must pass through the wires and through the device in order to reach the next device and, finally, to return to the battery. In this type of circuit, the wires run from the positive pole of the battery, through all the devices, and back to the negative pole.

A series circuit has some built-in disadvantages. The main one is that the current must run through all devices. If any device is not working, the entire circuit will be broken and none of the devices will work. Holiday tree lights used to be connected in a series circuit. Ask some adults if they remember having to search through all the lights on the tree to find the one that blew out. Until that dead bulb was found, none of the lights would work.

A series circuit also has a high electrical resistance. As you add bulbs to a series circuit, they become dimmer. Remember, the greater the resistance, the less current.

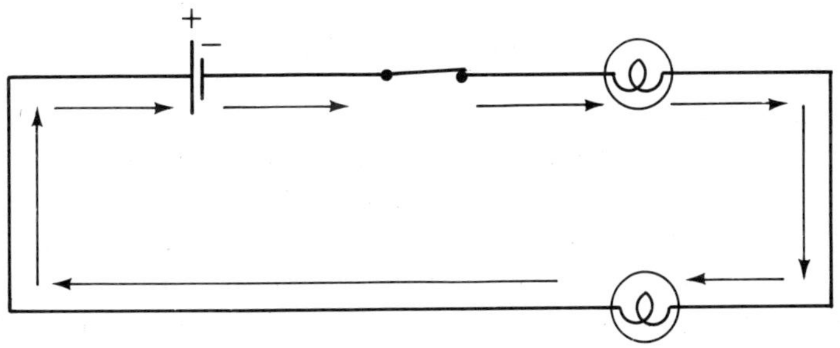


Fig. 5. Diagram of a series circuit. Arrows show electron flow.

## PROJECT 5:
## A SERIES CIRCUIT

MATERIALS

bell wire
6-volt battery
single-throw switch
two porcelain receptacles
two 6-volt bulbs

Strip the plastic insulator off both ends of all your plastic wire. Attach one strand of wire to the positive pole of the battery. Attach the other end of this wire to a single-throw switch. The switch, like the receptacles in the previous experiment, needs wires attached at both sides. Run a wire from the switch to a porcelain receptacle, from this receptacle to another receptacle, then back to the battery.

Once all the wires are connected, make sure the throw switch is in the open position. Next, screw in the light bulbs. Close the switch. What happens? Why? Unscrew one of the light bulbs. What happens? Why?

## PARALLEL CIRCUITS

A **parallel circuit** (Fig. 6) includes a number of electrical devices joined together by two wires and branches of these wires. Unlike in a series circuit, the current in a parallel circuit branches from the main wires to the electrical device, then returns to the main line.

Do you recall what happened when you removed a bulb from a receptacle in the series circuit? The other bulbs went out because the flow of electrons had been broken. This cannot happen in a parallel circuit, because electrons flow in two wires. Each bulb, or appliance, is connected by its own path; if a bulb is out, it only breaks the circuit along that path. It does not affect other bulbs.

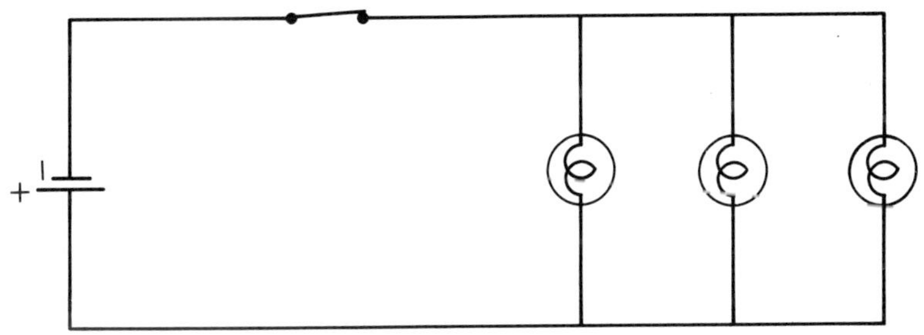


Fig. 6. Diagram of a parallel circuit

## PROJECT 6:
A PARALLEL CIRCUIT

MATERIALS

bell wire
three 6-volt bulbs
6-volt battery
three porcelain receptacles
single-throw switch

Strip the plastic insulator from the ends of the bell wire. Screw the bulbs into the receptacles. Follow Fig. 6 in making the rest of the connections.

Close the throw switch. What happens? Why? Unscrew one of the bulbs. What happens? Why?

Compare a parallel and a series circuit to see how resistance affects the brightness of the light bulbs.

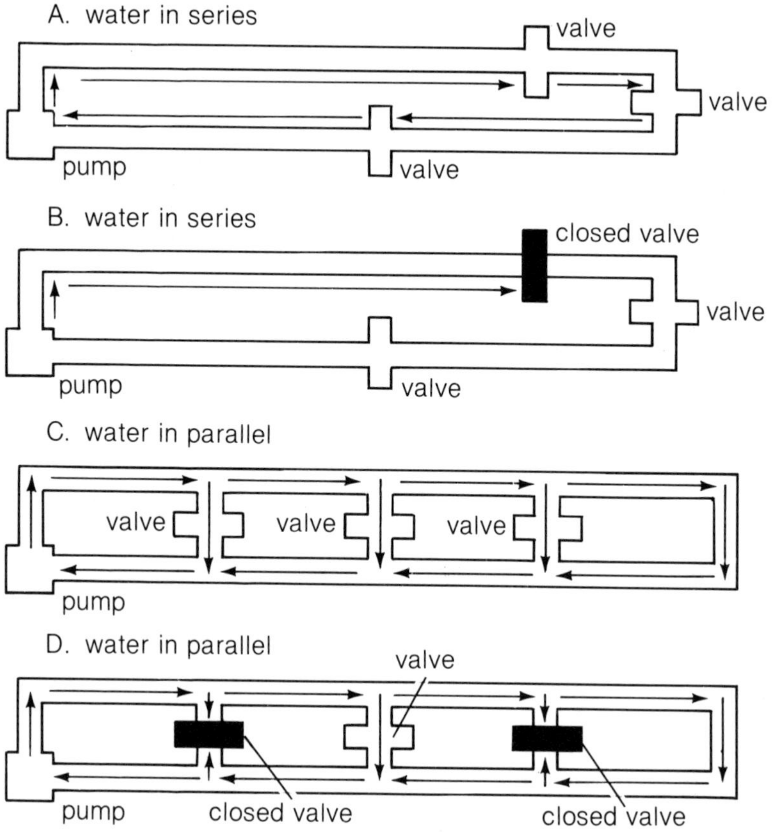


Fig. 7. These four drawings will help you understand circuits. Think of the pump as a battery and the valves as electrical devices. In A the water flows from the pump through each valve and back to the pump, making a complete circuit. In B one valve is closed, so the water cannot make a complete loop. It is a broken circuit. In C all the valves are open, creating open circuits. In D, with two valves closed, the middle valve and the pump still form a complete circuit. If the middle valve were an electrical device, it would work, even though the other two devices would not.

## WATER AND ELECTRICITY

The flow of electrons can be compared with the flow of water. In a water system, you have a pump and valves. Water systems can be constructed in both series and parallel circuits.

Water pumped in "series" (Fig. 7A) will follow the path of the pipes the way electrons follow the path of a wire. As long as all the valves are open, the water will be able to follow its designated route from start to finish. However, if one of the valves is closed (Fig. 7B), the flow of water is blocked to all of the valves and the water cannot complete its circuit.

Water pumped in "parallel" (Fig. 7C) follows two paths to complete its circuit. Each valve is connected by its own branch; it has its own path. If one of these valves is closed (Fig. 7D), the water bypasses that branch and goes on to the other branches. It can complete its circuit.

## A FEW QUESTIONS

Most of the world's electrical devices are composed of circuits. Will circuits be as useful in the future? What of computers? Do they use electric circuits? Can you imagine any type of electrical device operating without a complete circuit?

# 4

# ELECTRIC CELLS AND BATTERIES

## THE VOLTAIC PILE

As you have already learned, Alessandro Volta invented the voltaic pile, the world's first battery, in about the year 1800. The voltaic piles consisted of alternately stacked zinc and silver disks, separated by sheets of pasteboard moistened with saltwater. When the disks were connected by a wire attached to the terminals at the end of each pile, an electric current flowed through the wire.

Until Volta's discoveries, an electric current could be supplied only by static electricity machines. These machines were inefficient and could produce a current for only a short period of time.

Volta made it possible to produce an electric current that would last for a long time. The voltaic pile produced electricity for as long as the chemicals in the metals continued to interact.

The voltaic pile (Fig. 8) is an electric cell in which the **electrolyte** is a weak solution of hydrochloric acid and water. An electrolyte is a chemical solution that conducts electricity.

In a **voltaic cell,** the metal plates are known as *electrodes.* The acid in the voltaic cell acts on the metals, stripping away electrons from the atoms in one electrode. The electrons accumulate on the zinc plate. The zinc plate has now become negatively charged because it has an excess of electrons. The carbon or copper plate attracts positive charges and becomes positively charged.

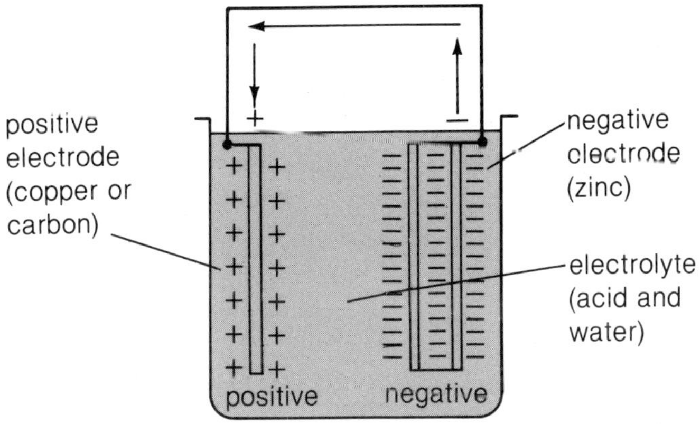


Fig. 8. In a voltaic cell, electrons flow from the zinc electrode to the copper electrode when the cell is part of a complete circuit. The electrons flow from where they are abundant to where they are not.

Electrons travel from a place where they are in excess to an area where they are lacking. Therefore, when a wire is attached to the two electrodes, the electrons in the wires flow from the negative pole to the positive pole. An electric current has been established.

The voltaic cell converts chemical energy into electrical energy. The zinc plate is the source of EMF. When the acid completely eats away the zinc, the battery no longer works.

## THE DRY CELL

The most common sources of limited electrical power today are **dry cells,** which are used to operate devices such as flashlights, calculators, and radios. The electrical output from a dry cell is limited. It is

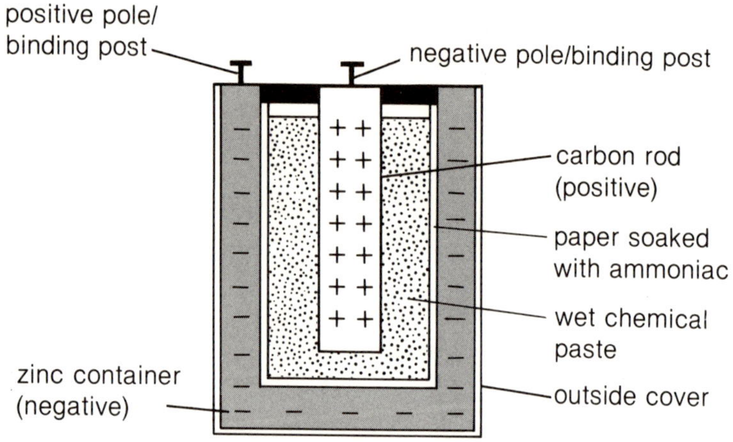


Fig. 9. Diagram of a dry cell

always 1.5 volts. Researchers are working on ways to manufacture stronger and more efficient dry cells.

A dry cell (Fig. 9) is tightly sealed with melted tar or sealing wax. This seal prevents the chemicals that cause reactions inside from drying up. All dry cells have a tightly sealed zinc container that lines the inner wall of the cell and acts as the negative electrode. The negative pole is usually on the top or bottom of the zinc container.

A carbon rod in the center of the dry cell acts as the positive electrode of the cell. On top of the carbon rod is the positive pole. The dry cell is filled with a wet, pastelike mixture of chemicals. Paper soaked in a special chemical separates the chemicals from the zinc container. As long as this paste remains moist, the dry cell will continue to function.

The carbon rod of the dry cell reacts with the wet paste mixture and loses electrons. This makes the carbon rod positively charged. The zinc reacts with the wet paste and collects free electrons. This gives the zinc a negative charge.

When the circuit is closed with a wire and some electrical device, the electrons are pushed from their excess (from the zinc container through the negative pole) to the place where they are fewer (to the carbon rod through the positive pole). As they flow through the wire, they enter the bulb and go through the filament. In the filament, the electrons encounter resistance, which causes the filament to glow.

## THE STORAGE BATTERY

The **storage battery,** or lead–acid cell (Fig. 10), also works on the principle of chemical action producing a flow of current. Chemical energy is transformed into electrical energy. Each cell of a storage battery is a single unit that usually puts out 2 volts. When the cells are connected in a series, they produce a greater voltage and are called a **battery.** The **amperage** stays the same, however, and is equal to the amperage of one cell. Amperage is a measure of the current—how much electricity moves through a circuit in a given time.

Storage batteries can be wet cells or dry cells connected in series. The cells are arranged so that the electric current flows from one to another. A three-cell battery would have 6 volts; a six-cell battery would have 12 volts.

The lead–acid storage battery consists of plates of lead peroxide, which serve as the positive pole, and plates of lead, which serve as the negative pole. A solution of sulfuric acid serves as the electrolyte. Each pair of plates is insulated by wood, rubber, or plastic separators.

When the battery is connected, electricity is produced as a result of the chemical reaction that takes place between the lead plates and the sulfuric acid. This reaction also causes a buildup of lead sulfate, a chemical compound formed as a result of the reaction

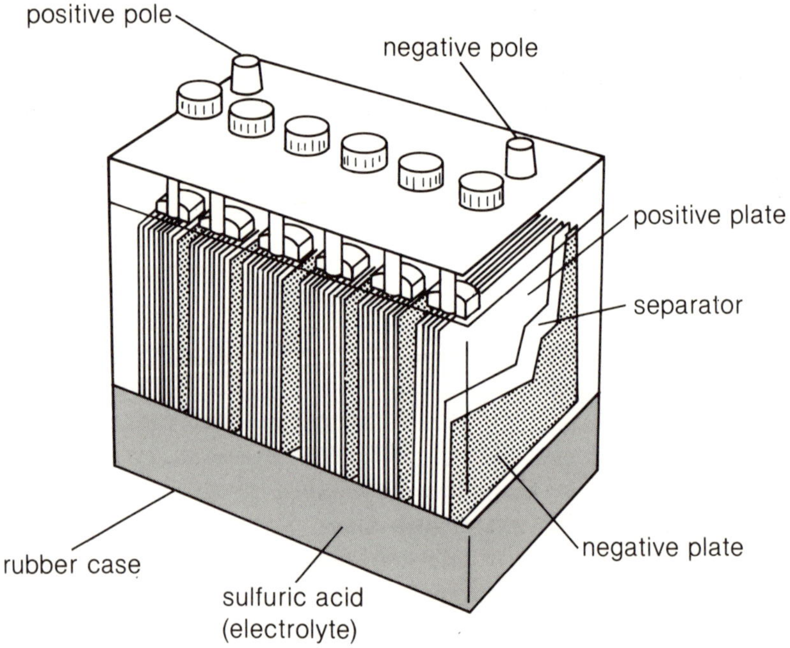


Fig. 10. Diagram of a lead–acid storage battery

between the electrolyte and the lead plates. As the lead plates become coated with lead sulfate, the battery loses power and eventually runs down.

Storage cells can be recharged by causing electrons to flow back into the cell. The ability to recharge a storage cell makes it one of the most useful of our electric cells.

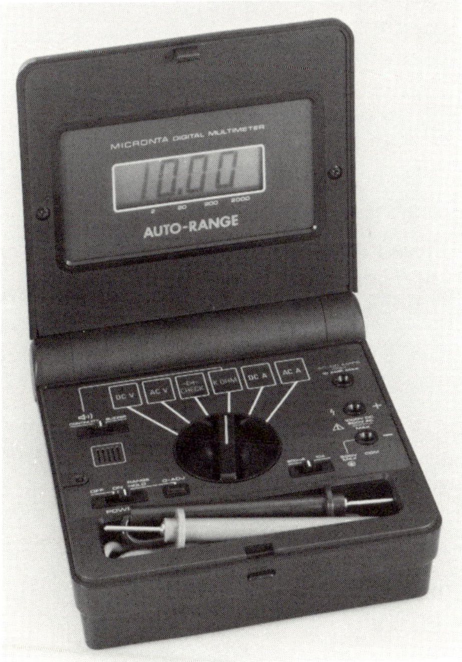


*(top) Four dry cells you probably are familiar with. (bottom) A meter that measures DC voltage (DC V), AC voltage (AC V), resistance in thousands of ohms (K OHM), DC current (DC A), and AC current (AC A). The meter also can tell whether a diode works (a diode converts AC to DC and is related to a transistor; see Chapter 9); —▷|— is the symbol for diode.*

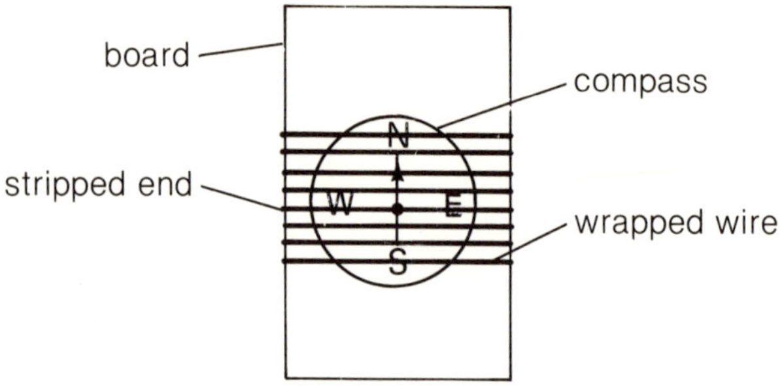


Fig. 11. Diagram of the galvanometer built in Project 7

## PROJECT 7:
## A GALVANOMETER

A **galvanometer** is a device that measures the flow of an electric current. It can determine whether an electric current is being produced. A galvanometer is important when working with batteries, because it can detect a flow of electrons too small to light a bulb or ring a buzzer. You will use this galvanometer in some of the following experiments with batteries. If electrons are in motion, the compass needle will jump.

MATERIALS

electrical tape
compass
piece of wood 3″ × 5″ (about 8 × 13 cm)
4′ (1.2 m) of bell wire

A galvanometer is simple to construct (Fig. 11). Roll a piece of electrical tape in a loop so that it is sticky on all its surfaces. Attach the tape to the bottom of the compass, then press the compass onto the center of the board. Strip the plastic insulator from each end of a 4-foot (about 1.2 m) section of bell wire. Wrap the wire over the compass and around the board. Wrap 2 feet (about 0.6 m) of bell wire to the right of the compass, and 2 feet (about 0.6 m) to the left side of the compass. Allow the stripped ends of wire to protrude from each end of the board.

## PROJECT 8:
## DRY CELLS IN SERIES

MATERIALS

bell wire
three 1.5-volt dry cells
6-volt bulb
porcelain receptacle
single-throw switch

Connect the dry cells and circuit according to Fig 12. This is a series circuit because the dry cells are connected negative to positive. Once all is connected, throw the switch. What happens? Now try the same experiment with only two dry cells. Throw the switch. Was there a difference in the intensity of the bulb? Remove yet another cell. Throw the switch. What is the difference, if any, from the three-celled circuit? Why?

Remember, when cells are in a series, they produce a greater voltage than any single cell. The voltage produced is equal to the sum of the voltage produced by three cells (1.5 + 1.5 + 1.5 = 4.5 volts).

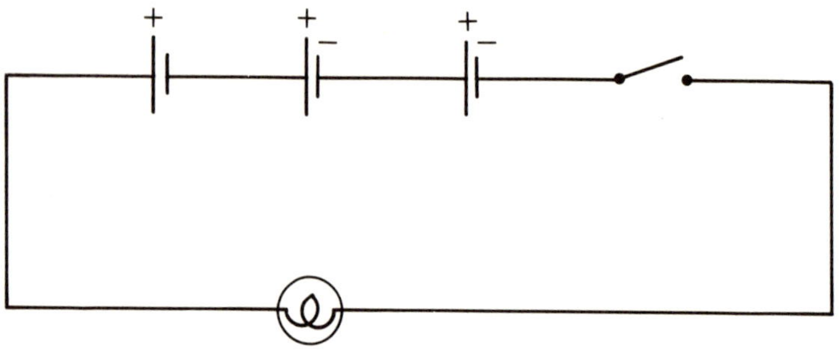


Fig. 12. Illustration showing dry cells connected in series, as described in Project 8

## PROJECT 9:
DRY CELLS IN PARALLEL

MATERIALS

bell wire
three 1.5-volt dry cells
6-volt bulb
porcelain receptacle
single-throw switch

Connect your dry cells and circuit according to Fig. 13. Repeat the experiment with cells in series (see Project 8) by removing a cell each time you throw the switch. Is there a difference in the intensity of the bulb? Why?

Cells in a parallel circuit provide the amperage equal to the sum of the current produced by the three cells. The voltage, however, remains the same as in one cell. This occurs because the voltage produced in any one cell depends only upon the chemical reaction

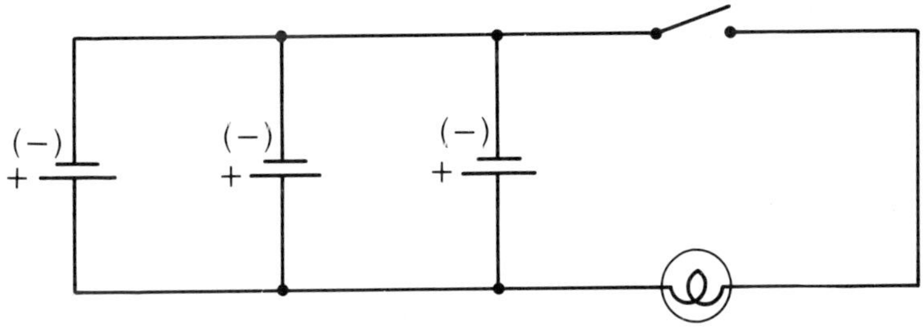

Fig. 13. Illustration showing dry cells connected in parallel, as described in Project 9

between the cell's electrodes and the chemicals within the cell. The size of the electrodes does not determine the amount of electrical pressure produced. Size determines how long the reaction or the cell will last.

In a parallel series of cells, the number of cells does not determine the pressure but, rather, how long the reaction will last. Cells in parallel last longer than cells in series.

## PROJECT 10:
## A WET CELL BATTERY

MATERIALS AND TOOLS

two empty pickle or mayonnaise jars
hand drill
two strips of zinc, 5″ (13 cm) long
two strips of copper, 5″ (13 cm) long

6′ (about 2 m) of bell wire
electrical tape
acetic acid (vinegar)
ammonium chloride
galvanometer
6-volt bulb
porcelain receptacle
single-throw switch

Wash the jars with soap and water and rinse well with warm water. Dry the jars thoroughly. Drill a hole at one end of each strip of metal. These strips of metal will serve as the electrodes for the battery. The copper strip will serve as the positive electrode, the zinc strip as the negative electrode.

Strip the plastic insulator from the ends of four strips of bell wire. Each wire should be about 18 inches (45 cm) long. Attach one end of each wire to each strip of metal. Do this by looping the wire through the hole and then twisting it to make a secure connection.

Place the electrodes in your empty jars. You may wish to secure them with electrical tape. The wet cell battery is all set now, except for the electrolytes.

Add acetic acid to one jar and ammonium chloride to the other. Run the wires from each electrode of the cell with the ammonium chloride to a galvanometer. Touch each wire to a wire on the galvanometer. What happens? Why? Do the same from the cell with the acetic acid. Is the reaction the same?

Using a light bulb, receptacle, and switch, set up a circuit using your ammonium chloride cell as the source of EMF. Do the same with the acetic acid cell. Is there a difference between the two cells as far as voltage is concerned? How do you know? Do some extra reading (see Bibliography) to see if you can learn why this is so.

Set up your two cells in series. Make sure you connect the right poles to each other. What are the results? Why? Set up your two cells in parallel. What are the results? Why?

## FOOD FOR THOUGHT

As you can see, the battery has come a long way since the time of the voltaic pile. What is the future of the battery? Today there are batteries, such as the nickel-cadmium storage battery, that last much longer than other batteries. There also are cells powered by the sun: solar cells. Will batteries ever become a practical means for powering an automobile? There are some electric cars today, but they are not yet efficient. Scientists are working on ways of making batteries better. Who knows what they will discover in the future?

# 5

# THE INCANDESCENT LIGHT

Throughout history, from the beginning of recorded time, people have been in search of better ideas for survival and convenience.

Many great discoveries and inventions were happened upon by accident. However, most inventions come about by the hard work of a person or persons using their minds to attempt to make living easier, more comfortable.

Such a man was Thomas Alva Edison (1847–1931), one of the best-known inventors of all time. Self-educated, Edison became interested in chemistry and electronics. His inquisitiveness caused him to experiment in both of these fields, and some of his experiments got him into trouble. One time he set a baggage car on fire while experimenting with a chemical, phosphorus.

Eventually Edison found a job as a telegraph operator in Mt. Clemens, Michigan. Among his duties was the task of reporting, by telegraph, to the city of Toronto, in Canada. He had to do this hourly. Edison viewed this reporting as a waste of valuable time, so he rigged up a time clock and attached a telegraph set to it. The time clock triggered the telegraph, and a signal was sent to Toronto hourly. This was Edison's first invention, and led to his spending almost all of his time working on other innovations.

Edison opened his first workshop in Menlo Park, New Jersey, where he developed many devices to help business and industry. Among these were improvements of the stock ticker, the carbon telephone transmitter, and the electric pen, which was used on the first mimeograph machine. Edison also contributed to film-making, and was instrumental in the development of sound movies.

One of Edison's most original inventions was the phonograph. He developed this idea while attempting to find a way to record telegraph messages.

The electric light was not Edison's idea alone. As he did with the telephone and the stock ticker, Edison found a way of making this device more practical. A Russian electrical engineer, Paul Jablochkov, had invented the arc light. The arc light used gas and was used only to light streets. It was in use as Edison worked on his incandescent light. Edison was looking for a light that could be used by everyone in their homes and in industries. In order to accomplish this, he needed to move away from gas as the energy source.

Edison's efforts finally paid off in 1879. After many unsuccessful attempts, he discovered a way to keep a filament glowing. He had tried almost every kind of material in his electric light, but nothing had worked. Finally, he tried carbonized thread, a thread coated with a carbon material. This, he thought, might work because it contained no oxygen. After many tries, he succeeded in placing the thread in a bulb. The bulb burned for approximately twenty-four hours. Eventually he developed a longer-burning bulb.

The **incandescent light** (Fig. 14) produces a bright and steady glow for many hours by means of electricity. The bulb itself has a positive and negative contact on its base. Wires run through the base and into the bulb. These wires, called lead-in wires, are attached to a filament usually made of tungsten. The bulb itself is generally filled with an inert gas, a gas that is chemically inactive, in order to keep oxygen out. Oxygen would extinguish the filament.

The filament in the electric light is usually a long, coiled, thin wire. This goes back to the idea of resistance. Remember, the longer the wire, the greater the electrical resistance. Also, the thinner the wire, the greater the resistance. Electrical resistance produces heat. As the electric current moves through the filament, free electrons bounce off the atoms. This creates friction and heat. The filament glows.

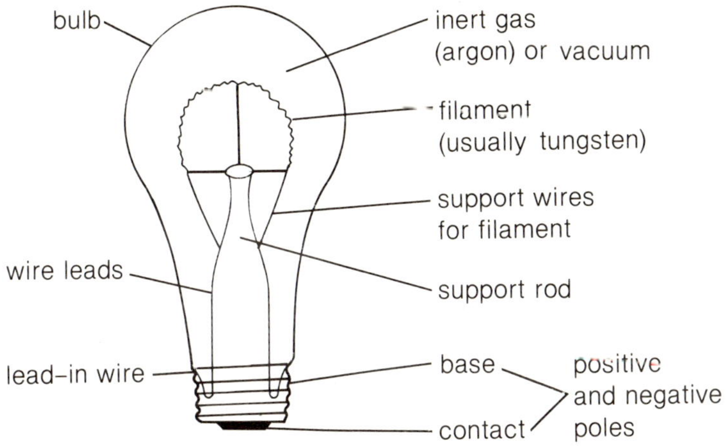


Fig. 14. Diagram of the parts of an electric light bulb

## OTHER LAMPS

The fluorescent lamp is much more efficient than the incandescent light. With the incandescent light, a great deal of energy is lost in the form of heat. The fluorescent lamp burns much cooler. While the incandescent lamp turns 6 to 8 percent of energy into light, the fluorescent lamp runs at 13 to 15 percent.

In the fluorescent lamp, the contact points at each end of the tube supply the current to the electrodes, which release free electrons inside the mercury-vapor-filled tube. These electrons cause

*Thomas Edison (right) reenacting the final process in the construction of an experimental light bulb in 1879.*

the vapors to give off rays, which cause a material called phosphorus to glow.

There are many kinds of light bulbs today. Lights are used for a variety of purposes, including lighting stores and homes, theatrical performances, movie sets, and greenhouses.

You may wish to investigate further the history of various lamps. Some lamps you may wish to find out about are the quartz tubular lamp, the sodium vapor lamp, and the neon light.

## PROJECT 11:
## AN ELECTRIC LIGHT BULB

MATERIALS AND TOOLS

awl
jar with lid
tungsten wire (if unavailable, use any thin wire except copper or silver)—a strand of picture-hanging wire works well
long, thin knitting needle or finishing nail
two steel nails
electrical tape
3′ (1 m) of bell wire
three 6-volt batteries

Use the awl to punch two holes in the lid of the jar. The holes should be just a little smaller than the steel nails and approximately 2 inches (about 5 cm) apart. Now coil the tungsten (or picture-hanging wire) around the knitting needle. Wrap the wire tightly so that there are many coils. REMEMBER, the longer the wire, the greater the resistance. Leave approximately ¾ inch (about 2 cm) of wire on each end of the coil.

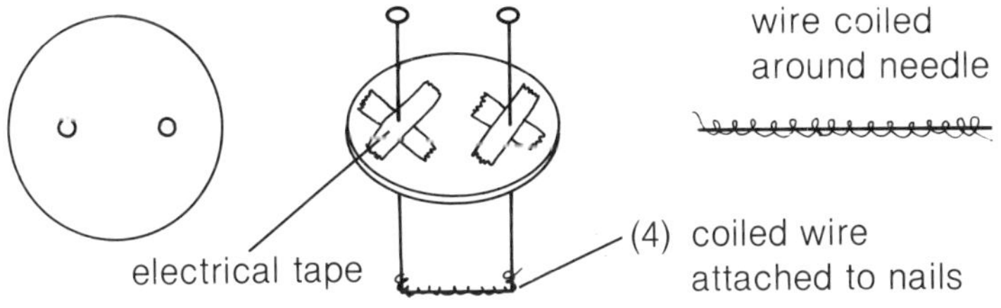


Fig. 15. Drawings of the cap and coiled wire for the light bulb built in Project 11

Tape the two steel nails through the holes in the lid of the jar. The heads of the nails should stand roughly ¼ inch (about 6 mm) above the lid.

This done, remove the coiled wire from the knitting needle and wind the ends around the pointed ends of the nail. Wind the coiled wire tightly to the nails. This will ensure a good connection. Put the cap on the jar and close it tightly. Use electrical tape and seal the lid of the jar. See Fig. 15.

Secure the nails in place with electrical tape. Put tape around the nail where it enters the lid of the jar. This will stop the nails from slipping.

Strip about 1 inch (about 3 cm) of insulation from both ends of two 10-inch (25-cm) pieces of bell wire. Attach the wires, one wire to each nail. Wrap each wire about the nail, under the head, and make sure there is a good connection. Hook up your circuit as shown in Fig. 16.

Close the circuit for only a short while and observe the result. Remember, Edison's light was filled with an inert gas in order to

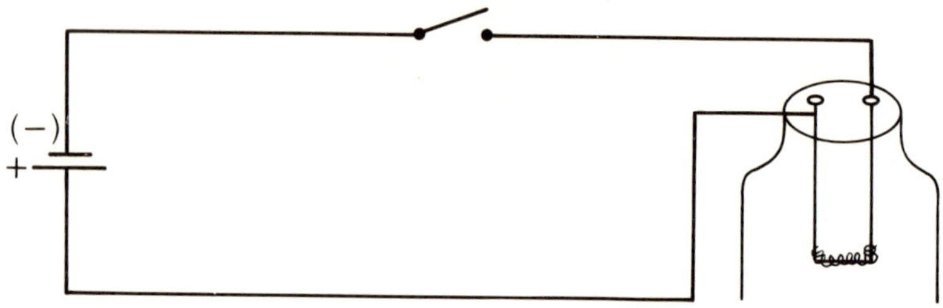


Fig. 16. Diagram of the circuit for the light bulb built in Project 11

prevent the filament of the light from burning through. Oxygen will cause the filament to burn rapidly and break.

Add another battery to your circuit. Close the circuit and observe the results. Was there a difference? Why? Now add a third battery. What happens? Why?

# 6

# ELECTROMAGNETIC DEVICES

**Electromagnetism** is magnetism produced by an electric current. A **magnetic field** resides in the space around a magnet, magnetic body, or electric current in which the magnetic force of the magnet or current is felt. The strength of a magnetic field decreases as you move away from the magnet. A magnetic field surrounds a moving electric charge and the wire through which an electric current is running.

Electromagnetism was discovered by the Danish scientist Hans Christian Oersted in 1819. Oersted discovered that an electric current would move a compass needle, just as you saw in doing Project 7. This showed him that an electric current generated a magnetic field. Oersted's discovery led to more discoveries about electricity and magnetism.

A French scientist, André Marie Ampère (1775–1836), discovered that there were forces between two wires carrying electric current. He showed that two parallel conductors carrying currents in the same direction attracted each other, while those carrying currents in the opposite direction repelled each other. Ampère concluded that an electric current generates a magnetic field that has poles. These magnetic poles conform to the magnetic **law of poles:** *Like* poles repel one another; *unlike* poles attract.

In 1821, Michael Faraday discovered that *magnetism could produce electricity.* He found that a conductor carrying a current would rotate about a magnetic pole, and that a magnetized needle would

MORSE CODE

| | | | |
|---|---|---|---|
| A | •— | T | — |
| B | —••• | U | ••— |
| C | —•—• | V | •••— |
| D | —•• | W | •—— |
| E | • | X | —••— |
| F | ••—• | Y | —•—— |
| G | ——• | Z | ——•• |
| H | •••• | | |
| I | •• | | |
| J | •——— | 1 | •———— |
| K | —•— | 2 | ••——— |
| L | •—•• | 3 | •••—— |
| M | —— | 4 | ••••— |
| N | —• | 5 | ••••• |
| O | ——— | 6 | —•••• |
| P | •——• | 7 | ——••• |
| Q | ——•— | 8 | ———•• |
| R | •—• | 9 | ————• |
| S | ••• | 10 | ————— |

rotate if near a wire carrying an electric current. Faraday also showed that a moving magnet could *induce,* or produce without direct contact, an electric current in a coil of wire. He made this last discovery in September 1831. This induced electric current, a current produced by a conductor rotating about a magnetic pole, is called **electromagnetic induction.** Most electrical devices work on this principle of an electric current being induced by magnets and wires.

Joseph Henry, an American, also worked on electromagnetic induction at about the same time as Michael Faraday. After making many electromagnets, Henry came upon the idea of operating electromagnets at a distance. This was a significant thought in the development of long-distance communication. In 1831, he successfully operated two electromagnets connected by a line 1,030 feet (314 m) long. This was the prototype of the telegraph.

The first practical telegraph was built by Samuel Morse in 1844. Electromagnetism makes possible the operation of this simple device.

A simple telegraph system contains a sender and a receiver, which are identical but serve opposite functions at the same time. When the telegraph key in the sender is depressed, an electric circuit is completed and a current is transmitted through wire to the receiver. The current activates an electromagnet, which then causes a mechanism to click.

When the key is depressed for just an instant, the sound received is a "dot" in Morse code. When the key is depressed a little longer, the result is a "dash." Using Morse code, which assigns different combinations of dots and dashes to the letters of the alphabet and to numbers, you can send messages.

The person on the receiving end, having exactly the same setup as the person on the sending end, can reply to the message. The receiver is now the sender.

Today most telegraph messages are not sent using telegraph keys. Instead, sophisticated electronic equipment is usually used, which automates the process. You might want to see if you can find anyone in your community who still uses a telegraph key to send messages.

# 7

# ELECTRIC MOTORS AND GENERATORS

## ELECTRIC GENERATORS

It was Faraday's discovery of electromagnetic induction that led to the development of the modern electric generator. A generator produces electricity because a conductor moving through a magnetic field generates electricity.

Electric generators produce almost all the electricity used by people. Without these machines that change mechanical energy into **electrical energy,** our economy would be at a standstill. Industries would have to shut down, and households would have no electric lighting, refrigerators, or other major appliances.

A generator works on mechanical energy, energy produced by machines. The mechanical device that moves the generator is called a **prime mover.** The prime mover supplies the mechanical energy that is then transformed into electrical energy. The prime mover may be a steam engine or a diesel engine. It could be a windmill. In an automobile, the prime mover is the car engine.

A simple generator consists of a permanent magnet and a loop of wire (rotating conductor). The conductor must have a connecting link to an outside circuit. When the rotating conductor (the wire loop) interrupts the magnetic field, an electric current flows through the wires.

The magnet is called a **field structure** because it creates a magnetic field. The wire loop is called an **armature.** The connecting link to an outside circuit is made of slip rings and **brushes.** See Fig. 17.

As the armature moves, it interrupts the magnetic field and creates an electric current; the current flows through the wire to the slip rings. The slip rings are attached to the armature shaft. Brushes, usually carbon, are attached to the slip rings and to an outside circuit. The electricity reaches its outside goal through the brushes.

The armature is always turning and thus interrupts the magnetic field downward and then upward or, if you prefer, right and left. Because of this, the current changes direction with each turn of the armature. The change in direction against the magnetic field reverses the current.

When the armature is straight up and down, no current is produced. The most current is produced when the armature is parallel between each magnet. The current produced in this manner is called **alternating current,** or **AC.**

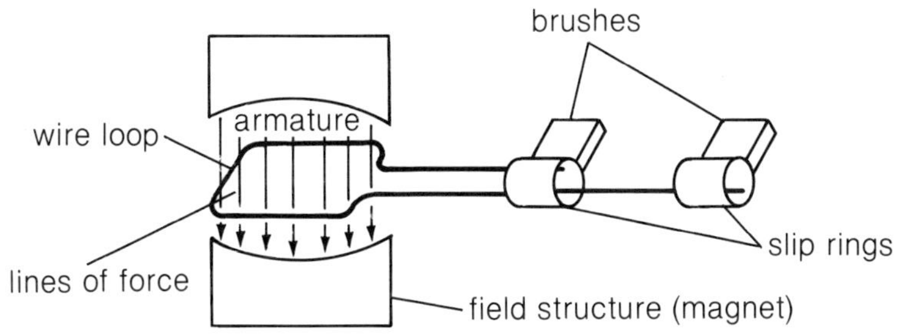


Fig. 17. The armature and brushes of an electric generator are illustrated here.

There are also **direct current,** or **DC,** generators. Direct current generators cause the current to move in only one direction. This is done through a device called a **commutator.** The commutator

*Armature winding of a generator at an electric power station. See if you can find some other generators to compare with this one, for example, a bicycle-light generator or a car generator (your local gas station probably has some car generators you could look at).*

changes the AC inside the generator to DC as it travels out of the generator. This type of current, because it is steady, is best for automobiles, ships, and locomotives.

The giant generators that power our cities and industries work on the same principles as our simple AC generator. The major difference between the two is that in the large generators the field structure is an electromagnet that turns inside the armature. The armature is stationary, and the field structure turns.

Electric power plants use coal, oil, or water for many of their large generators. Coal is burned in a furnace and used to heat water until it turns to steam. The steam turns large blades of a turbine (prime mover). The turbine is connected to the shaft of an electromagnet (field structure) and causes it to turn inside the stationary armature. The spinning of the field structure produces electrical energy: AC. Electric power lines that run to industries and homes are connected to the generator. The power that runs into homes lights rooms, runs devices, and sometimes heats the house.

## ELECTRIC MOTORS

An **electric motor** works like a generator in reverse. A generator turns mechanical energy into electricity. A motor, on the other hand, turns electricity into mechanical energy.

The force that causes an electric motor to move is produced when two magnetic fields meet. The first field is that of the armature. Both the armature and the **field structure**—the magnets that create the magnetic field for the armature to cut—in an electric motor are electromagnets (Fig. 18). The armature rotates between the poles of the field structure. This is accomplished by the north pole of the field structure attracting the south pole of the armature, and the south

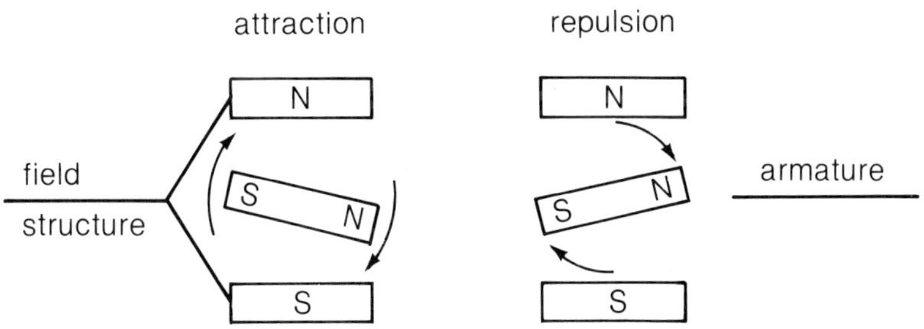


Fig. 18. Drawings of the field structure and armature of an electric motor

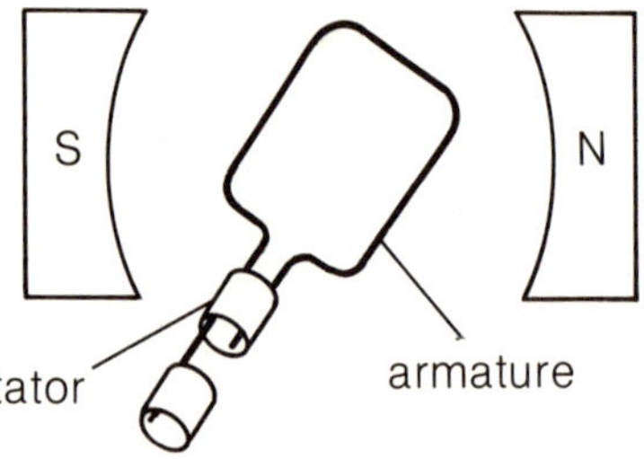


Fig. 19. Illustrated here are the commutator, field structure, and armature of an electric motor.

pole of the field structure repelling the south pole of the armature. This attraction and repulsion causes the spin.

Electric motors also contain a commutator (Fig. 19), which changes the current in the armature so that the unlike poles do not stick together. Just as the armature is about to bring a south pole and a north pole together, the commutator changes the polarity of the armature so that the poles are alike and the armature is repelled.

The commutator is constructed of two split rings. They are attached to the armature and rotate with it. The rings are split into two equal sections and conduct electric current to the armature through brushes attached to each ring.

As the armature turns, so do the split rings of the commutator. When the poles of the armature are next to the opposite poles of the field structure, the commutator switches terminals and reverses the current. Positive becomes negative, and negative becomes positive. Because of this, the armature always keeps turning in the same direction. See

A generator produces electricity. An electric motor uses electricity to produce mechanical energy. In a generator, brushes take the current to an external circuit. In an electric motor, brushes bring the current into the armature. In a generator, the commutator makes the current flow in one direction. In an electric motor, the commutator switches the current so the armature will turn in one direction.

Electric motors today are used to run many different devices, such as refrigerators, can openers, garage door openers, and a host of other devices. Electric motors run fans and furnaces, as well as garbage disposals and trash compactors. Although these motors vary in style and size, they all work on the same principle as the motor designed in this chapter.

The first usable electric motor was constructed in the 1880s. Today, electric motors are found in every aspect of our daily lives: homes, schools, businesses, government, and industry. Without them our standard of living would not be as good as it is now.

# 8

# THE TELEPHONE

Alexander Graham Bell (1847–1922) invented the telephone with a little help from the contributions of other scientists and inventors.

Although he was born in Scotland, he did most of his important work in the United States. In Boston, Massachusetts, Bell searched for a way of sending many messages at once over a telegraph. His researches led, in 1876, to the first understandable transmission of a human voice over a telephone.

## HOW IT WORKS

When the vibrations from a person s voice enter the **transmitter** of a telephone (Fig. 20), they set up an electric current that is carried over a wire to a receiver. The transmitter contains a thin metal disk sensitive to sound vibrations. This metal disk, called a **diaphragm,** vibrates when struck by sound.

The diaphragm is connected to a cup filled with tiny grains of carbon. A loud sound pushes the grains tightly together and makes it easier for an electric current to travel over the wire. The grains remain less compact with softer sounds, making it more difficult for the current to travel over the wire. These carbon grains make it possible to mimic the exact sound of the voice. The sound waves themselves do not travel through the wire.

The **receiver** is made of a diaphragm that vibrates when an elec-

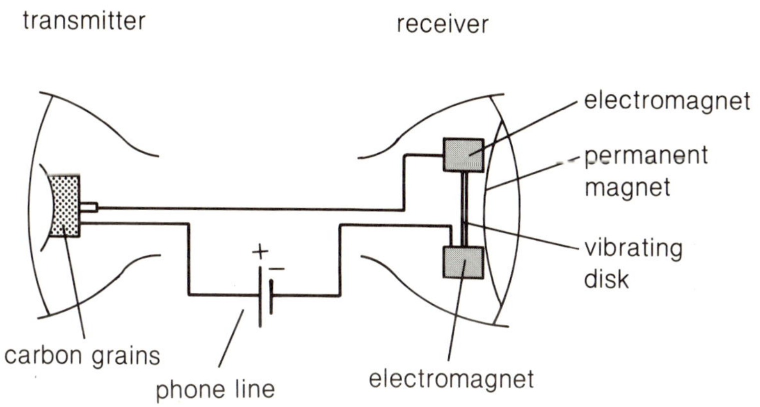


Fig. 20. Diagram of a telephone

tric current passes into it. Two magnets on the side of the diaphragm cause it to vibrate. One of the magnets is a permanent magnet (a magnet that is always magnetized); the other is an electromagnet (a magnet that is magnetized by an electric current). The permanent magnet keeps the diaphragm in place and in close proximity to itself. The electromagnet controls the vibrations of the diaphragm by pulling it away from or pushing it toward the permanent magnet.

When you speak into the transmitter of a telephone, the voice patterns cause the carbon particles to change the *resistance* in the circuits. This resistance controls the amount of current passing through the wires. According to the amount of current, the electromagnet in the receiver becomes weaker or stronger and either pushes or pulls on the diaphragm. This vibration occurs at the same frequency as the sound waves that enter the transmitter. Therefore, the human voice is almost exactly duplicated.

*Alexander Graham Bell speaking into the "Centennial" telephone. This telephone may not look like your telephone, but it works in a very similar fashion.*

Your telephone is part of a worldwide network communications system. When you make a call, the signal travels to a switching station. Here, the switching apparatus connects your telephone to the telephone at the number you are calling. All this happens with amazingly rapid speed.

As you pick up your telephone, a dial tone signals that the circuits are clear to handle your call. Dialing your number breaks the current, and an electric signal goes to electromagnets that connect you to the number you have dialed.

Over one hundred million telephones are in use all over the world, and over half of these telephones are in use in the United States alone. Who would have thought that in just over one hundred years the art of communication would have come this far?

## PROJECT 12:
## A SPEAKING TUBE

The earliest "telephones" were tubes that captured sound waves and directed them to a certain place. By directing the sound waves, these tubes stopped the waves from spreading in all directions. The results were that the waves, because they were traveling in only one direction, were stronger and went further.

These speaking tubes were not used to communicate over great distances, but they were effective over short distances, for example, from the front to the rear of a house, or from downstairs to upstairs. Here's how you can build a speaking tube.

MATERIALS

Long, flexible tube (could be vacuum cleaner hose or wide-mouthed, rubber tubing) long enough to reach from one room to another room

Obtain long, flexible tubing from a hardware store or a junkyard. If you get your tubing from a junkyard, clean it thoroughly before using it for this experiment.

Hold one end of the tube, having another person go into a difffrent room holding the other end of the tube. Have this other person hold the end of the tube to his or her ear. Whisper some message into the tube. You may have to try this several times to achieve the proper voice level.

After your message has been delivered, switch the tube to your ear so you can hear the other person's response. Remember, this primitive telephone system works because it allows sound waves to travel in only a single direction.

## PROJECT 13:
## A WIRE TELEPHONE

Here are plans for another simple telephone.

MATERIALS AND TOOLS

two empty tin cans
25′ to 100′ (about 8 to 35 m) wire (picture frame wire is good)
small drill or punch (awl)

Wash out the tin cans, drying each thoroughly. Punch, or drill, a hole in the bottom of each can. Push the wire through the hole in each can, and tie a knot in the end of the wire so that it will not come out of the can. Pull the wire to test if the knot holds.

Test the telephone with another person. Have the other person take one of the tin cans and walk as far away from you as the wire will stretch. The wire must be stretched tightly for the telephone to work.

Speak into your tin can. When you speak into the tin can, the can becomes a diaphragm. The other person puts the second tin can to his or her ear. That person's tin can becomes the receiver.

As you speak into the diaphragm, your voice will cause the diaphragm to vibrate. These vibrations will travel over the wire to the other tin can. The bottom of that second tin can will pick up the vibrations from the wire, and the person should be able to hear what you have said.

# 9

# ELECTRONIC DEVICES

Televisions, radios, and computers are devices that work on the principle of **electronics.** Electronics deals with flowing electrons, or electrons in motion. When the electron moves, it has energy that can do work.

As you will recall from your study of the atom, the electron is the moving part of an atom. These moving electrons sometimes fly out of their orbit and move away from the atom. When they do this, they are called **free electrons.** Free electrons do not belong to any particular atom. Electronic devices control the flow of these free electrons.

## THE VACUUM TUBE

One device used to control the flow of electrons is the **vacuum tube** (Fig. 21). A filament is heated by an electric current so that it gives off electrons. As the electrons escape from their atoms, a positive electrode (the anode) attracts them, and a negative electrode (the cathode) repels them. Magnetic fields are used to deflect the electrons as they travel through the vacuum in the tube. Two magnets can be made to create an **electric field.** An electric field not only deflects electrons but also can speed up or slow down their movement.

When a vacuum tube is part of a complete circuit, the electrons flow through the wire to the cathode, move across the tube to the anode, then exit the tube and move on to the next part of the circuit. The tube alters the current in some way, depending on its purpose.

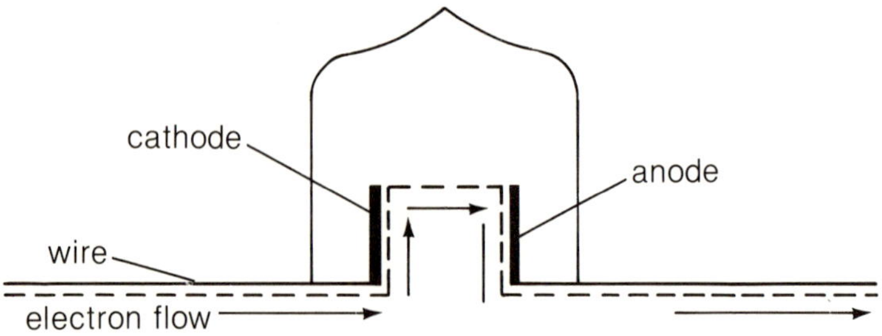


Fig. 21. Diagram of a vacuum tube, showing the flow of electrons

Perhaps it speeds up the electron flow, or perhaps it changes the direction of the flow. Whatever the tube does, the electrons, when they leave through the anode, are altered or have been altered in the tube.

There are many types of vacuum tubes, and many types of jobs they can do. For example, they can rectify the current, or change alternating current to direct current. They can amplify the current, or take a small amount of current and increase it to a large amount. And they can convert one form of electrical energy into another, for instance, into X-rays or radio waves.

## TRANSISTORS

In 1947, after years of research, three scientists working at the Bell Telephone Laboratories invented a device containing a crystal of the element germanium that amplified a telephone voice in the laboratory forty times. These scientists had invented the **transistor,** a very small electrical device that could do many of the same things a vacuum tube could do, and could do many more things as well. They received the Nobel Prize in 1956 for their work.

*(left) A vacuum tube.*
*(top left) A transistor.*
*(top right) A new computer memory chip (the dime shows its relative size), which contains the equivalent of thousands of transistors. However, this chip can do things no quantity of old-fashioned transistors or vacuum tubes could do.*
*(above) Computer chip, showing its circuits.*
*The tube, transistor, and "chip-on-a-dime" are all shown lifesize.*

Explaining how transistors and similar devices work is beyond the scope of this book. You might want to read some of the books listed in the Bibliography at the end of this book to find out more about transistors.

Transistors have many advantages over vacuum tubes. Vacuum tubes are large and bulky, break easily, and are slow in warming up. Transistors are small (today's transistors are microscopic), almost unbreakable, and "warm up" instantly.

Because transistors are solid materials and tubes contain a vacuum, transistorized devices are referred to as *solid state,* which indicates they have no tubes.

Because transistors can be made so small and do not heat up, they can be enclosed in a very small space. When transistors were first invented and then applied to devices, the size necessary for these devices was shrunk. For example, a portable radio that used to weigh 25 pounds (11 kg) could be made to weigh less than a pound (0.5 kg).

Today, transistors can be so small that a microscope is necessary to see them. Tens or hundreds of thousands of transistors can fit into one **microchip** no bigger than the eraser on a number 2 pencil. Transistors packed together in a tiny chip form an **integrated circuit.** An electronic device may have many integrated circuits connected by *etching,* not wires. Etching is like scratching on the surface, or a groove.

Integrated circuits are found in televisions (along with a vacuum tube—the picture tube), radios, tape recorders, cameras, automobiles, aircraft, computers, satellites, space shuttles, and other products. A whole computer can now be put on a single microchip. Calculators can fit on the face of a watch, and radios can be found the size of a fat credit card—well, almost!

# EPILOGUE

The Earth has developed in stages. At various times, different types of plants and animals have populated its surface. Humankind, too, has developed in stages. Each age centers around a central feature of the way people have manipulated tools and their environment.

In the Stone Age, early human beings developed stone tools and implements to help them adapt to their surroundings. The Bronze and Iron Ages followed. During these latter two periods, people learned ways to use bronze and iron to improve their lives.

Yet, of all the various periods that people have proceeded through, none yet has had the impact or originality of the Electrical Age. The discovery and development of a new force, electricity, has changed our ideas of the universe, enabling us to do things never before dreamed possible. Electricity has extended human control over the environment. It has made instant communication possible, and has made our world seem a much smaller place.

# GLOSSARY

Alternating Current (AC)—An electrical current in which the electricity flows regularly in one direction and then the other, reversing many times per second. Most electrical generators produce alternating current.

Amber—A yellowish fossil resin that the early Greeks believed to have magnetic qualities.

Amperage—The strength of flow of an electric current.

Anode—The positive (+) pole of an electron tube or battery. Negatively charged ions are attracted to the anode.

Armature—The rotating conductor on a generator. The armature rotates and passes through a magnetic field in order to produce electricity.

Atom—A small particle that makes up matter. All atoms have a positively charged nucleus, containing protons and neutrons, and negatively charged orbits, consisting of moving electrons.

Battery—Any object that produces free electrons through chemical action.

Brushes—The part of an electric motor that carries the current from the commutator to the connecting wire.

Cathode—The negatively (−) charged pole of an electron tube or battery. Positively charged ions are attracted to the cathode.

Circuit—The complete path, or part of it, through which an electrical current flows. An electrical circuit consists of an electromotive force (EMF), a conductor, and an electrical device.

Closed Circuit—Any electrical circuit in which the electrons are allowed to flow through the conductor because the switch is closed.

Commutator—A device that changes alternating current inside a generator or motor to direct current as it travels out along its circuit.

Conductor—Any substance which has the ability to transmit an clcc trical charge.

Current—The flow of electrons from one point in a conductor to another.

Current Electricity—Electric current flowing from an EMF source through a complete circuit.

Diaphragm—A thin disk, in a telephone receiver, which vibrates on electric impulse to transmit sound.

Direct Current (DC)—An electrical current whose electrons flow in one direction.

Dry Cell—The major source of limited electrical power today. Consists of chemical pastes and metals that interact to produce electricity.

Electrical Energy—A form of energy created by moving electrons.

Electric Field—A force field of electrons that can be created by two magnets. This type of field deflects electrons.

Electric Motor—A motor that operates on the principle of electromagnetic rotation.

Electrolyte—A chemical solution that conducts electricity.

Electromagnetic Induction—Producing an electric current by moving a conductor through a magnetic field or moving a magnetic field close to a conductor.

Electromagnetism—Magnetism produced by electric current.

Electromotive Force (EMF)—Any force that causes an electric current to move through a conductor. The current moves because the EMF possesses excess electrons. These excess electrons flow to a place of fewer electrons.

Electron—The only moving part of an atom, possessing a negative (−) charge and moving in orbits around the nucleus.

Electronics—The study of electrons in motion.

EMF—See *Electromotive force*.

Field Structure—The permanent magnets in a generator that create a magnetic field. The armature moves inside the field structure.

Filament—A long, coiled, thin wire found in an incandescent lamp. This wire creates electrical resistance and glows as electrons pass through it.

Free Electrons—Electrons that do not belong to any one atom. These are the electrons that flow through a conductor. Conductors have many free electrons.

Galvanometer—An instrument used for measuring an electric current.

Generator—A device that converts mechanical energy into electrical energy.

Incandescent Light—A type of bulb that produces light at a high temperature.

Insulator—A poor conductor of electricity.

Integrated Circuit—A circuit consisting of a lot of smaller circuits "integrated" together on one microchip.

Law of Electrostatics—Unlike electrical charges repel each other; like electrical charges attract each other.

Law of Poles—Like poles of a magnet repel; unlike poles attract.

Leyden Jar—An early device for storing electricity. A glass jar lined with foil inside and out, closed with a stopper, and with a brass rod connected to the stopper and foil.

Lodestone—A naturally occurring magnet.

Magnetic Field—The space around a magnet or electric current in which the magnetic field can be detected.

Microchip—A small integrated circuit used in many electrical devices.

Ohm's Law—The larger the resistance, the smaller the current. The greater the EMF, the greater the current.

Open Circuit—Any electrical circuit in which the circuit is broken and the electrons cannot travel from start to finish.

Parallel Circuit—Includes a number of electrical devices joined together by two wires and branches from these wires.

Prime Mover—The mechanical device that moves the turbines of a generator.

Receiver (telephone)—Contains an electromagnet that vibrates a metal disk.

Resistance—Quality of a circuit or electrical device that opposes—or resists—the flow of electricity.

Series Circuit—Includes two or more electrical devices joined by wires along a single path.

Static Electricity—Electricity at rest. Usually a large number of electrons in one place, not flowing as current.

Storage Battery—Chemical action used to produce a flow of electrical current. Chemical energy is converted to electrical energy.

Transistor—A small device that does everything a vacuum tube does—and more.

Transmitter (telephone)—Contains carbon particles that move and alter the flow of electrons in order to produce electrical impulses that relay sound.

Vacuum Tube—A device that controls the flow of electric currents.

Volt—A unit for measuring electromotive force.

Voltaic Cell—The first battery in which the electrolyte changed chemical energy to electrical energy. Invented by Count Alessandro Volta.

Voltaic Pile—A combination of zinc and copper disks stacked, with an electrolyte paste between, to create electromotive force. Invented by Alessandro Volta.

# BIBLIOGRAPHY


Ardley, Neil. *Discovering Electricity.* New York: Watts, 1984.

Asimov, Isaac. *How Did We Find Out About Electricity?* New York: Walker, 1973.

Bendick, Jeanne. *Electronics for Young People.* New York: McGraw-Hill, 1973.

Bleaney, Betty I. and B. *Electricity and Magnetism.* New York: Oxford, 1976.

de Lucenay Leon, George. *The Electricity Story.* New York: Arco, 1983.

Dunsheath, Percy. *Giants of Electricity.* New York: Crowell, 1967.

*Electronics.* Boy Scouts of America. Irvington, Tex.: 1977.

Epstein, Sam and Beryl. *Electricity,* rev. ed. New York: Watts, 1977.

Grob, Bernard. *Basic Electronics.* New York: McGraw-Hill, 1977.

Hintz, Sandy. *Computers in Our World, Today and Tomorrow.* New York: Watts, 1983.

Marcus, Abraham and William. *Basic Electricity.* Englewood Cliffs, N.J.: Prentice-Hall, 1974.

Math, Irwin. *Morse, Marconi, and You: Understanding and Building Telegraph, Telephone, and Radio Sets.* New York: Scribner's, 1979.

Math, Irwin. *Wires and Watts: Understanding and Using Electricity.* New York: Scribner's, 1981.

Morgan, A.P. *The First Book of Radio and Electronics for Boys and Girls.* New York: Scribner's, 1977.

Owers, L.W. *Electronics: An Elementary Introduction for Beginners.* Philadelphia: International Ideas, 1978.

Ruchlis, Hyman. *The Wonder of Electricity.* New York: Harper & Row, 1965.

Vogt, Gregory. *Electricity and Magnetism.* New York: Watts, 1984.

Wheeler, G. J., and Tripp, A. L. *Essentials of Electronics.* Englewood Cliffs, N.J.: Prentice-Hall, 1971.

# INDEX